Money Life & You

**Financial Planning, Pre & Post Marital
(A Christian Overview)**

Dr. Donald A. Nurse

EdD, PCC, CFP(cert.)

Money, Life, & You

Financial Planning – Pre & Post Marital

(A Christian Overview)

By

Dr. D. A. Nurse, EdD, PCC, CFP (cert.)

Abundant Life Institute

4151 Route 130 South, Edgewater Park, NJ 08010

(856) 461-7000

Money, Life, & You

Financial Planning – Pre & Post Marital

(A Christian Overview)

© Copyright by Dr. Donald A. Nurse, December 2013

All rights reserved. This book may be reproduced in portions for teaching or sharing, but no part may be sold without the explicit permission of the author.

Scripture references are from the King James Version (KJV) of the Bible.

Cover & Back Designs by:
Marlon Nicolls & Associates
www.marlonicolls.com

Also by Dr. Donald Nurse:
Managing God's Finances
www.createspace.com/3991925
www.amazon.com

CreateSpace ISBN – 13:978-1494984007.

Printed in the United States of America

REVIEWS

Dr. Nurse's latest publication is a must-read for everyone. He offers a unique approach to guiding the reader through a number of financial land mines. There is a lot to grasp regarding how to handle money efficiently. He provides sound guidance about ways to achieve the financial security that all of us seek, especially during these desperate economic times in our nation.

He explains with great clarity the financial terms and systems that the average person may not know. Dr. Nurse laid the financial groundwork for anyone seeking to understand finances. As a marriage consultant, it will be a must-read for my clients.

Dr. Milton Bradley
Bradley Consultation Firm

Dr. Donald Nurse has done an exceptional job addressing this much needed and crucial area, associated with Money, Life, and You – the individual and couples alike, thereby the marriage and family; Pre, Post, and beyond. It helps to bring individuals and couples face to face with giving serious attention to areas often overlooked and which can serve to strengthen the marriage or result in that family's destruction. Families are so often destroyed for a lack of integrity relating to finances and issues of trust.

This work not only causes some serious introspection and internal reflection on the part of individuals and couples alike, but it provides the necessary tools for undertaking a thorough investigation of areas which so often after the fact have proven to be what should have been considered in the beginning.

I applaud Dr. Nurse for undertaking the challenge to help men and women (Families) to understand what it will take to build a solid foundation causing the marriage to last and endure the obstacles which we call life.

Dr. Maurice Randolph Sr. M.A.T.S., D.P.C., BCPC
Senior Pastor, Marriage & Family Counselor,
Board certified Pastoral Counselor

In Money, Life and You, Dr. Donald Nurse sets forth a valuable and much needed Christian perspective on the management of money and wealth. He addresses an old and persistent view that God prefers His people to be poor and in order to be holy.

Because of this view, many faithful believers have experienced unnecessary hardships. They suffered not so much because of their faith, but because of a lack of knowledge. At times the pendulum of thought swings to the other extreme by advocating flawed versions of a "prosperity Gospel." Both extremes require correction.

In Money Life and You, Dr. Nurse forthrightly addresses this issue. He makes it very clear that it is God who gives the power to acquire wealth. He also explains the reason why God gives anyone the ability and opportunity to gain wealth. When God makes a covenant with persons or nations, it is always His will that they have the resources necessary for the fulfillment of that covenant. That is the powerful assertion of Deuteronomy 8:18 and 2 Corinthians 9:8.

It is God's desire that His children have sufficient for every good work. Therefore creating and managing wealth is indispensable to us becoming and achieving what God wants us to become and what He wants us to achieve. Having sufficient must become a living reality, and not just an inspiring but tantalizing aspiration.

This understanding is critical for those who are in the early stages of planning a life together. It can spare them indescribable anguish in their relationships, and help them to establish a firm financial foundation for their lifelong journey.

Dr. Nurse also offers excellent advice for those who are already married at whatever stage of adult life they happen to be. He details valuable guidance and specific instructions that can help anyone to improve their financial situation as well as other areas of life that are all too dependent upon healthy finances.

Money, Life, and You is indeed a valuable resource for young people as well as for the more mature. It is for those who want to govern their financial lives in ways that honor God, work to their advantage, and for the benefit of those who are engaged in life with them.

Apostle Abraham Fenton
Founder & Overseer
Abundant Life Fellowship Church

Money, Life, & You – Financial Planning, Pre & Post Marital.
(A Christian Overview)

'Money, Life and You' is not a book that one will read through once and then leave on a shelf. It is a guide to help couples through all the stages of their lives. Founded on sound scripture it underscores the need and benefits of being good stewards of God's blessings. And, although it reveals the importance of starting early, the financial advice is sound at any stage of life. I have been married for 40 years and I found that there are things we can incorporate into our own financial life right now. Just as with one's relationship with Christ - it's never too late to start!

Rev. Barbara Duguid, BTh, MDiv
A Minister of the Presbyterian Church in Canada

ACKNOWLEDGEMENT

The email simply requested a return call. Little did I realize that I was about to engage one of the foremost passions of my life – a passion fueled by the doctoral program I attended at Argosy University. My Executive Pastor at Abundant Life Fellowship Church, Rev. Aubrey Fenton, sought my willingness and availability to aid with premarital counseling as it pertained to financial matters.

This booklet was conceived as a direct result of our discussion. It is therefore with sincere gratitude that I acknowledge Pastor "Aubrey's" trust and delegation of such an important task to me. The preparation of this booklet speaks of an approach committed to the excellence demanded of such a venture.

Finally, none of this would be possible without the presence and guidance of the Holy Spirit – thank You Lord. He must have spoken to my wife too, she is always supportive and provides invaluable suggestions – thank you GB. Loving every moment of this journey!

Dr. D.A.N

INTRODUCTION

I believe that there are three inter-related phenomena that affect human behavior, positively or negatively - depending on individual orientation and experience. One's **SPIRITUAL** persuasion will have an impact on self, and the relationship with others. Consequently, **INTIMACY** at all levels can also be influenced by the Spiritual. **MONEY**, which at first glance seems isolated from the other two areas, can be a buffer or serve to cause a strain on the relationship. Some of the words of a famous Caribbean song tell it all, "…. No money, no love!" A more serious description from an unknown source indicates that *money rings the warning knell of disaster*.

It is my assumption that you are reading this book because you desire to avoid the financial pitfalls and curved balls that life throws at us from time to time. Common sense demands that we examine ourselves, and our current position in order to make necessary adjustments. However, the question is, "When should I begin to plan for my financial stability?" There is no one answer to this question. Nevertheless, this booklet attempts to isolate some common financial issues by targeting the agents of the Family

Structure, male and female, prior to their marriage (Pre-marital), and also touch on some Post-marital challenges.

I must make it clear that this is not a panacea for all financial issues. This booklet simply identifies and introduces some financial strategies to help couples begin the plan for their financial security. Individuals are advised to seek a professional financial adviser if greater financial details and guidance are desired.

LIST OF CONTENTS

Part A.

Pre-Marital Financial Plans:

1. Some Spiritual Considerations. — 13
   a. Consider the Origin of Wealth. — 13
   b. The Original Financial Plan. — 14
2. Honesty – An Imperative. — 18
   a. Individual Net Worth. — 20
   b. Legal and other Liens. — 23
3. A Pre-Marital Covenant. — 24
4. Wedding Plans – A Financial Test. — 26

Part B.

Post-Marital Financial Plans:

5. Budgeting - Revisited. — 31
6. Investing. — 35
7. Insurance Planning. — 40
8. Estate Planning. — 46
9. Retirement Planning. — 51
10. Taxation – General. — 56

Epilogue — 65
Bibliography — 68

PART A
Pre-Marital Financial Plans

Chapter 1

SOME SPIRITUAL CONSIDERATIONS

Consider the Origin of Wealth.

    Regardless of your spiritual or religious persuasion, you must admit that at some time in your life the question pertaining to *the origin of things* crossed your mind. Scientists in search of the "truth" have attempted various explanations – including the Darwinian theory of evolution. Yet, none has managed to present an explanation that defies any refutation.

    The Christian experience however, seems to be the only avenue that offers a direct solution. It is backed by the evidence of accurate prophetic announcements made thousands of years ago – some of which have been verifiably fulfilled, while others are unfolding before our very eyes – the current trouble within the world's economic system being one of them. Archaeological discoveries also continue to corroborate the content of important Biblical texts. What then can we learn about the origin of wealth from this source – the Scriptures? This is not a trivial question – the answer, or your perception of it, may very well play an important role in the success or failure of your financial endeavors.

In the Beginning. According to the Gospel of John, chapter 1 and verse 3, as well as Hebrews chapter 11 verse 3, God made *everything*. We should therefore have no objection when He says in the Book of Haggai chapter 2 and verse 8 that both the silver and gold are His. The possession of these precious items has always been viewed as a measure of one's wealth – each can be converted to liquid cash when necessary. Nevertheless, there remains a lingering question! We have addressed the origin of wealth – God made, and consequently owns all that He made – everything, including elements of wealth. It is evident that many individuals possess (not own) silver or gold, or their monetary equivalent. What then, is God's purpose for such a distribution of His wealth? The answer can be found by examining the original financial plan.

The Original Financial Plan.

God began His relationship with us by bestowing a great blessing through Adam and Eve. The Edenic Blessing, Genesis Chapter 1, verses 26 – 28, represented God's trust in our ability to be excellent stewards of His creation. The entrance of sin corrupted this plan for our economic security. Ever since that time, God sought someone who would be faithful in their relationship with Him, and who understood their stewardship responsibilities. Abraham, considered the father of faith, was such a man. Subsequently, his descendants, the nation of Israel, served to demonstrate the right and wrong ways of implementing God's financial plan. We will draw from some of their experiences.

The Tithe.

This is perhaps the single most controversial financial issue that has caused much dissension among families. There is no intention to deal fully with this topic here – that would require an independent booklet. Suffice it to say that tithing serves to demonstrate our obedience to God's commands, positions us for a continuous flow of God's benevolence, and aids us with our budgetary considerations – it demands good stewardship.

Money, Life, & You – Financial Planning, Pre & Post Marital. (A Christian Overview)

The Financial Trail. When we examine the life of Abraham, we discover that his obedience to God's call, resulted in the acquisition of much wealth – God was the first to give. The Edenic Blessing was flowing once more. Later, in Genesis chapter 14 verses 17 – 20, we read of tithing for the first time. Abraham's descendants saw the economic benefits of this system. So, 430 years later, Moses incorporated it formally through the Levitical Law (Lev. 27:30-34). Here we learn that the tithe represents 10% of all new increases, and is holy unto God – it belongs to God. In the last Book of the Old Testament, Malachi (chapter 3 verses 8 – 12), we get a definitive look at God's personal view concerning this instrument of worship and obedience. These verses leave no doubt that God intends to bless us (empower us to prosper) continuously. Jesus reaffirmed the need to tithe (Matt. 23:23; Luke 11:42), and continues to receive tithes from us as our heavenly High Priest, always interceding on our behalf (Hebrews 7:1-28). But why does God desire to share His wealth with us?

Israel, Our Example.

The period between their exodus from Egypt, and settlement in the Promised Land, made the Hebrew people a perfect example of God's financial plan at work. They left Egypt with great wealth – although they had been slaves for 430 years. This can be described as the greatest wealth transfer ever recorded - Egyptian masters to freed Hebrew slaves (Ex. 12:35, 36).

Secondly, on the night of that first Passover, something supernatural transpired within the Hebrew community – miracles of healing. They were protected by the blood on the door posts and, together with the roasted lamb – atypical of the shed blood of Jesus and His body on the Cross, the transformation occurred.

So, while there was death all around them in the Egyptian camp, there was a renewal of life in their environment. Psalms 105:37 declares that there was not a single feeble person among the Hebrews as they left Egypt that night – a miracle.

Misuse of God's Funds.

God funded the Exodus with exceptional excellence and foresight. The Jews had money to pay for the various necessities as they travelled through the desert over 40 years. But some of the baser sort moved to rebel against the God who saved them from bondage. They fashioned another god with some of the wealth entrusted to them – a blatant misuse of God's funds. They paid the ultimate price (Ex. 32:1-33).

Remember Jericho! It is evident that greed can cloud the heart - obscuring the benefits of obedience. Joshua strictly warned the Israelites that the 'spoil of war' taken from their first victory in the Promised Land, was actually a 'First Fruit' offering to God in its entirety. Yet, Achan (head of a family) thought he could steal what belonged to God. The result, he brought a curse upon the entire camp of Israel until his covetous act was discovered. ***He, his entire family, and all his possessions were destroyed***. The tithe is holy, and belongs to God as an integral aspect of our covenant (Josh. 6:16-19; 7:1-26).

God's Purpose for the Wealth.

The Tabernacle. Now there were those who recognized the goodness of God, and were determined to obey His directions. So, when Moses, following God's instructions, offered them the privilege of co-laboring with the Almighty toward greater fellowship, they willingly participated. The building of the tabernacle in the wilderness, and Israel's willing contribution (materials and labor) to its successful completion, demonstrate two things; the lavish extent of God's blessings when Israel 'spoiled' the Egyptians, and His continuous benevolence to those who are honest stewards of His resources (Ex. 35:1-35). The Golden Candlestick (Menorah, made of pure gold) alone, weighing approximately 67 pounds (using the lowest weight calculation, Babylonian), would today be worth $1.5 million (Ex. 25:31-39). It is God's desire to bless those He can trust with His wealth.

The Legacy of Abraham. When God called faithful Abraham into service, He made a promise that remains significant to this day. The Lord told Abraham that through him, ***all families*** of the earth would be blessed (Gen. 12:1-3). Moses gave us a clear indication of God's ultimate purpose for the wealth. Deut. 8:18 is, without question, a direct disclosure of the ***Source*** of our wealth, and the ***Reason*** based on a unique ***Covenant*** with God. Gal. 3:13,14, 29 alert us to our position as heirs of Abraham through Jesus – ***Abraham's legacy is now ours!*** Consequently, that means the families remaining to receive the ***Blessing*** of ***Redemption*** will be impacted by <u>our</u> actions - particularly, by our dedication to the 'End Time Harvest' fund. So then, it is imperative that we make every effort to be debt free, remember that the tithe belongs to God, and use the wealth He gives us to help ***missions***, and other ***evangelistic*** programs as directed by the Holy Spirit. ***This is the true and ultimate purpose of the wealth!***

Chapter 2

HONESTY – AN IMPERATIVE

SOME QUESTIONS TO CONSIDER BEFORE MARRIAGE

The following are some examples of simple questions that most couples fail to address prior to marriage. Later, when individual sentiments are made known, it may be too late for remedial action. The best approach is to identify potential conflicts of interest while there is time to make relevant adjustments – that is, before the wedding:

Q 01. How large a wedding do you desire – private, small, medium or large?

    A. ………………………………………………

Q 02. How will the wedding be funded – Our parents or our own funds together?

    A. ………………………………………………

Q 03. Do you wish us to rent or own our home?

    A. …………………………………………….

Q 04. Where do you wish to live, State/City?

    A. ……………………………………………..

Q 05. Do you wish to raise a family? If yes, how many children do you desire? A. ………………

Q 06. If the answer to Q 05 is yes, how soon do you wish to start a family? A. …………………………………………………..

Money, Life, & You – Financial Planning, Pre & Post Marital.
(A Christian Overview)

Q 07. Do you have any plans for further education?

A. ………………………………………..

Q 08. When last did you file Federal and State Income Tax Returns? A. ……………………………….

Q 09. Do you have any outstanding debt?

A. …………………………………………………….

Q 10. Do you know your Net Worth (what you own minus what you owe)?

A. …………………………………………………….

Q 11. What are your views about gifts to the Church?

A. …………………………………………………….

Q 12. What are your views about the tithe?

A. …………………………………………………….

Q 13. What are your views about the *Lotto* and other *Games of Chance*?

A. ……………………………………………………..

Q 14. Do you have any physical or medical challenges?

A. ………………………………………………………………………..

Q 15. Do you have health insurance? A. ………………………………………..

Q 16. Are you challenged by the request to answer any of these questions? If so, which? A ……………………………………………………..

Each of these questions has a bearing on the direction of your financial affairs. The honest reflection and answers should pave the way for a healthy relationship that begins with trust, and a commitment to sound economic practices. Reject the mindset:

"Until <u>DEBT</u> do us part."

Individual Net Worth.

The decision to enter into a covenant of marriage must of necessity *follow* some vital considerations. For example, each individual should have a concrete perception of what the ideal marriage would be like, and consequently the ultimate goal for the union. However, to achieve the desired end, the current situation must be ascertained – you must know where you are in order to adopt appropriate means to get to where you wish to be.

Germaine to this presentation is the inevitable position that, whether the consideration is intangible (peace of mind), or tangible (a healthy bank account), money will have an impact on the decision making process. Your **Net Worth** is the vehicle to arrive at your current financial health. This is simply the total value of what you *own* minus the total value of what you *owe* others. Below is an example of what it should look like:

What You Own (Assets)	Dollar Value
Cash, Cash Equivalent	
Checking Accounts	$ ....
Money Market Accts.	....
Savings Acct.	....

Money, Life, & You – Financial Planning, (A Christian Overview) — Pre & Post Marital.

  Certificates of Deposits   ……………..

  Life Insurance (cash surrender value)   ……………..

  Stocks   ……………..

  Bonds   ……………..

  Govt. Securities   ……………..

  Mutual Funds   ……………..

  Equity – Own Business   ……………..

  Other Investments   ……………..

What You Own (Assets contd.)   **Dollar Value**

Retirement Funds

  Pension (current value) $……………..

  Joint & Survivor Annuities   ……………..

  IRAs & Keogh Accts.   ……………..

  Employees' Saving Plan (such as a 401K)   ……………..

Real Estate

  Your House   ……………..

  Other Properties   ……………..

Other Personal Property

  Household Furnishings   ……………..

Special Items
(car, boat, jewelry, tools) ....

Miscellaneous Property ....

Total Assets $ ....

What You Owe (Liabilities)

Charge Acct. Balances ....

Credit Card Balances ....

Auto Loans ....

Other Personal Loans ....

Mortgages ....

Home Equity Loans ....

Life Insurance Policy Loans ....

Other Liabilities ....

Total Liabilities $ ....

Estimated Net Worth (Assets minus Liabilities)

Total Assets $ ....

Minus -

Total Liabilities ....

Net Worth $ _____

NOTE: Use the current Fair Market Value for items where actual value is not known i.e., what would you sell it for now, not what you paid for it.

This step, arriving at your individual Net Worth, enables both parties to understand the financial climate or obligations that the marriage would begin with. It sets the stage for an honest and open relationship – money matters!

Legal and other Liens.

The careful preparation of the Net Worth statement should serve to list any legal or other liens that exist. However, the ego can influence the retention of embarrassing particulars. For example, Court decisions for Child Support, repossession of items such as cars, the repayment of Guarantor loans (Obligated to repay a loan as guarantor when the primary party failed to live up to their obligation), as well as personal loans and financial arrangements for which there is no official record.

Individuals may believe that such disclosures could tarnish their prospects of cementing the union. It actually demonstrates the desire for total honesty, and should rather serve as a catalyst for a perpetual bond.

Chapter 3

A PREMARITAL COVENANT

A covenant is in essence a binding contract between two or more parties. It can be as simple as a vocal agreement in the presence of witnesses, or formally written to ensure that there is no variation to the salient features over time.

There are particular requirements for a viable covenant, regardless of its format, vocal or written. Essentially, a covenant should comprise of three things:

1. **Words** of the Covenant – what each party agrees to fulfill as terms of the covenant.
2. The **Seal** of the Covenant – The Rings in a marriage ceremony, a Handshake, or the Signatures of primary participants.
3. The **Sacrifice/Memorial** – Blood (consummation of a marriage), Salt – the symbolic mixing of some salt from each party, indicating that, like the mixed salt, there is no possibility of future independent identification and consequently, no possibility of separation – the couple is viewed as one unit.

The serious and irrevocable nature of the process illustrated above would suggest (for the purpose of this booklet), that each person is obligated to the other for a **candid declaration of their commitment to proper monetary stewardship**. Toward that end, a **Premarital Covenant** should serve to draw attention to the importance of financial matters within the marriage.

Money, Life, & You – Financial Planning, Pre & Post Marital.
(A Christian Overview)

At this time each person should be aware of the Net Worth of the other. Therefore, all financial obligations have been recognized. The Premarital Covenant simply acknowledges whatever monetary commitments exist (if any – this excludes recurring expenses such as food, gas etc.), and establishes a shared undertaking to eliminate all outstanding debt. This can be a simple vocal declaration, or reduced to writing for a continual reference to the commitment.

The foregoing has not been easy. However, if you have attained a closer relationship as a result of applying these principles, it bodes well for a stable future – emotionally and economically. There remains one final premarital challenge – planning for the wedding.

Chapter 4

WEDDING PLANS – A FINANCIAL TEST

We are now positioned to make a careful assessment of crucial and pertinent elements that can determine the course of the union. It would be prudent to pause for a reflection on the areas covered so far. We are aware of the following:

1. God is the Creator and owner of all that exists.
2. We know the origin of wealth.
3. We know God's purpose for the wealth – that it is ultimately to help fund the End-Time Harvest of souls.
4. We know the results of misusing God's wealth as well as the rewards for being excellent stewards – God's relationship with Abraham and the experiences of Israel are our examples.
5. We know the importance of the tithe.
6. We know that honesty is imperative for a successful union.
7. We have shared our individual Net Worth – we know our current financial positions.
8. We have engaged a Premarital covenant – committing to proper financial stewardship after marriage.

The next important consideration revolves around the actual wedding. Planning for this 'LIFE' event can be the most stressful experience so far.

Wedding Plans

There are several areas that need careful attention – planning for the appropriate date, church, auditorium, number of guests, music, and cuisine, to name a few. Since this booklet concerns the financial aspect of such plans, it should be noted that every area depends on the availability of adequate financial resources.

Engaging a financial plan for any occasion is actually to Budget for it – that is, to be aware of the magnitude and consequent financial implications of a proposed event. It also demands knowledge of the actual financial resources available to cover the occasion. The various and necessary requirements for the successful completion of the event, as well as the individual cost for each must be known as well. Finally, it must be ascertained whether the available resources are enough to meet the need. Remember, the goal is to be debt free – ideally, the cost of the wedding should be met in full without the need to incur debt. What a great way to begin the marriage.

Based on the foregoing, the first decision should concern the size and type of wedding – should it be a wedding confined to immediate relatives, or elaborate enough to involve relatives and friends from both parties? This may depend on who is funding the event – parents, or the couple themselves? The following is a list of items for a simple Wedding Budget:

TYPICAL WEDDING BUDGET

Available Funds $ ………..

Required Items   Cost

01). Wedding Dress $ ………..

     Alterations   ………..

02). Tuxedo/Suit (Groom)   ………..

    Alterations   ………….

03). Other clothing (Bride)   ………….

04). Other clothing (Groom)   ………….

05). Wedding Bands/Rings   ………….

TYPICAL WEDDING BUDGET (CONTD.)

06). Flowers & Decorations   ………….

Church (donation, choir)   ………….

07). Invitations & Postage   ………….

08). Transportation (limousines) ………….

09). Auditorium (rent)   ………..

    (including valet parking and custodial services – coats, hats)

10). Cuisine (catered)

    …. Guests X $…. per head=   ………….

11). Bar/Beverages   ………….

12). Wedding Cake   ………….

13). Entertainment:

    Orchestra/DJ   ………….

14). Honeymoon (travel/hotel) ………….

15). Provision for tips (general) ....

16). **Sub-Total of all expenses** $..............

17). Add 10% of sub-total for

　　　Contingencies　　　　　　..............

18). **Total wedding expenses** $...........

Assessment:

19) Available Funds for the wedding $..........

20). Less Total Expenses -　　　　............

21). Balance　　　　　　　$..........

　　　It is needless to say that the communication, honest discussions, and general agreement between the two individuals are crucial to avoid over expenditure. *Wedding debt can affect the financial viability of a marriage for years after the occasion.*

CONGRATULATIONS! YOUR DILIGENCE IN COMPLETING THIS FINANCIAL REFLECTION ESTABLISHES A FIRM FOUNDATION FOR THE APPROPRIATE ATTITUDE AND RESPONSE TO FUTURE ISSUES IMPACTING YOUR ECONOMIC WELL BEING DURING MARRIAGE. MAY GOD BLESS YOU RICHLY AS YOU ADHERE TO HIS RULES OF ENGAGEMENT FOR _HIS_ FINANCES.

PART B

Post-Marital Financial Plans

Chapter 5

BUDGETING – REVISITED

During the previous section there was an example of a simple budget – planning for the wedding. It presented a great opportunity to practice for more complex situations. The principles remain the same, but there are other items that should be considered. This chapter will highlight further area to enable the satisfactory completion of any budget, regardless of its complexity.

Let Us Bake A Cake.

I like using this approach because most persons will identify with it – one way or another. You may be someone who loves to bake, and so this becomes very familiar, relevant and pertinent. You must have consumed a slice of cake at some time, and wondered how it was made. Regardless, the following illustration should make it easy to identify the rudiments of proper budgeting.

Principle # 1 – A Budget is a Plan.

Once the decision is made to bake a cake, several things must be considered: what kind of cake it will be for instance, which in turn then determines what ingredients will be necessary.

Principle # 2 – Document the Entire Process.

It should be easy to list the main ingredients for any cake – flour, sugar, butter, to name a few. But sometimes we may forget the small items such as salt and baking soda - these too are essential. Documenting the process helps to minimize the prospect of an incomplete *list* and hence afford the accurate *pricing* for the entire venture.

Principle # 3 – Cost each Item.

The heart of the budget is to ascertain the cost for the project. This is achieved by pricing each individual item, and adding their costs together. It is imperative that *current* market prices are used. A wise gesture would be to add 10% of the total cost to the budget. This serves as a cushion in anticipation of unexpected contingencies such as a change in prices.

Principle # 4 – Verify The Availability of Adequate Funds to Complete the Project.

This is where discipline becomes crucial. When funds are inadequate, either postpone or cancel the project. In some instances, the project may still be viable if it is scaled down – bake a smaller cake! No one should build a house without first counting the cost (Luk. 14:28-32).

Principle # 5 – Monitor All Expenditure.

It would be a futile effort if the hard work done previously is ignored when purchases are made. The expenditure for each item must be monitored to ensure that the cost within the budget is maintained.

Principle # 6 – Review the Plan.

Our example – baking a cake, gives a great illustration of the need to review the financial plan. Once we purchased the ingredients through the accuracy of our price list, we can mix and bake the cake.

It would appear that we have covered all relevant financial angles. But have we? What about the **OVERHEAD** costs for items such as the gas or electricity needed to bake the cake, what about the fuel utilized to go shopping for the ingredients? This may seem to be nit picking, but can prove disastrous if omitted from a larger project. *Bottom line – ensure all costs are included, regardless of an apparent lack of significance.*

A regular Family Budget.

The importance of budgeting cannot be over emphasized. Most families wish to enjoy a stable financial environment. This is achieved through careful financial planning – especially if practiced consistently from the inception of marriage. The following are some areas peculiar to the regular family budget:

1. List all sources of income and the amounts. This should include but not limited to wages, Income Tax refunds, and gifts.
2. You should know your monthly expenditure, and the related items. Remember to list the small non-essential items such as that daily 2nd cup of coffee. A safe method is to log all expenditure over a three months period, and divide the total by three to arrive at your average monthly expenditure.
3. Next, create a realistic financial plan that ensures no excess spending beyond the income mentioned at 1 above. This may mean foregoing that daily 2nd cup of coffee, and other non-essentials.

4. The final, yet perhaps most important consideration – ensure that your budget includes an amount for *Tithing* and *Personal Savings*.

An Overview.

Generally speaking, the same principles used to budget for a cake can be utilized in any situation. A budget simply serves to identify and cost the various items necessary to engage a project. It functions to compare the total cost of the venture with the funds available to complete it.

A successful budget paves the way for other important financial considerations. The wise investment of available resources can be beneficial for short or long term plans. This includes things such as purchasing a car, a home, or planning for retirement. Such a wide scope of benefits dictates a more in-depth look at Investing. This is our next area for discussion.

Chapter 6

INVESTING

I once heard someone say that true wealth is not determined by what you have in your possession, but rather by your ability to use it to create more substance. Money is currency and needs to flow – it needs to work for you – *you* should not be working for money!

The above views are likely to prompt a Christian person to ask in the customary quizzical way, "Do you have Bible for that?" I do. Examine Jesus' parable of the talents (Matt. 25:14-30), note verse 27 in particular. Jesus is actually saying that the unprofitable servant, *should have invested the money in order to gain interest on it.* It is obvious therefore, that each of us should seek ways and means to invest. However, experience has shown that many Christians are like the unprofitable servant – reticent about taking the necessary *risk*. I believe this is due to the traditional misrepresentation of God's views on wealth – people were made to believe that it's all right to remain poor, that it portrays holiness. Christian education is now reversing this unbiblical and negative thought pattern.

Some 'experts' consider investing as a *Discipline,* while others see it as a *Science*. Yet, there are those who claim that it is an *Art*. I can understand the various perceptions because I view it as a combination of all three! One needs *Discipline* to remain committed to the enterprise for the long haul. One also needs to be aware of the historical data that reflect the economic trends of a particular instrument over time – *Science*. Finally, one must develop the *Art* of making wise choices between the various instruments available for investment purposes. This should be based on scientific data, as well as other pertinent and relevant information.

The imbedded truth of previous paragraphs illustrate that, contrary to some Christian beliefs, investing is **not** *gambling*. Gambling depicts a conscious or subconscious attraction to *greed* – Jesus would never advocate such behavior! Rather, it is a means by which an individual can legitimately generate wealth for future use. The following is a list of the basic principles governing investing. These represent a simple introduction to this vital area of financial planning for life's journey. Greater details are always available through individuals qualified to offer professional financial guidance.

The Portfolio.

There are numerous instruments available for investment. One can invest in the stock of a company, in oil, in precious metals, in real estate, just to mention a few of the various vehicles. When one invests in several of these instruments, the items are together known as your portfolio. The general idea is to follow the principles mentioned previously - purchasing each instrument at the lowest cost with the conviction that, according to market trends, it will increase in value. Therein lies the need for discipline, a study of market trends, and the art to select profitable devices. The long term will surely bring a profit.

Risk Tolerance.

Every venture has some degree of risk – some more than others. Likewise, the tolerance for risk taking varies from individual to individual. The combination of psychological and natural factors create a *Risk Tolerance Level* for each person.

Money, Life, & You – Financial Planning, Pre & Post Marital.
(A Christian Overview)

Basically, the younger you are, the more risk you are likely to entertain. This tolerance diminishes with age – individuals become progressively averse to risk, especially as one approaches the time to retire. It should be noted that the greatest risk brings the greatest return, less risk, less return. Why is this important? This knowledge helps you to maintain a *Balanced Portfolio* in order to minimize losses while maximizing the potential for growth.

A Balanced Portfolio.

Let us examine some basic and general instruments for investment, while fashioning a *Balanced Portfolio* in the process.

The Savings Account. This is the safest one can get. Consequently it pays the least on your investment. One needs to shop around to acquire the best rate.

The Certificate **of Deposit.** This is also known as a *CD* or *Time Deposit Account*. It differs from the regular savings account because it stipulates a time frame. During this period you will not have access to your funds unless you pay a penalty. The rate of return is a little higher than the regular savings account.

The Money Market Account. This is the most aggressive bank instrument with relative safety. It requires a particular amount for deposit. It differs from other instruments in a unique way – your money is pooled with other deposits and invested. The beauty is that the bank creates a portfolio – *they, not you,* monitor the total investment. The return is usually far better than the two other saving instruments mentioned previously. Note that the investor always has access to the current balance – once the minimum deposit is retained. Many banks also provide checks to allow the ease of transactions from the account.

Mutual Funds. One of the greatest ways to invest, especially if you are not skilled at personally developing and monitoring your portfolio. This investment is similar to the Money Market Account – pooling funds of various investors, but requires a larger initial investment. Nevertheless it is simple enough to allow small investors to experience the same privileges and benefits normally enjoyed by more experienced investors.

Your investment allows you to gain access to experienced managers who make decisions on your behalf – they *Diversify* your portfolio to ensure growth over time; they send you annual statements showing the performance of your investment; and they structure your investment according to your *Risk Tolerance Level*. Finally, along with the potential for growth over time, you always have access to your funds – your investment is marketable, and therefore can be sold. Again, your success hinges on your ability to be disciplined, and to exercise patience – growth is guaranteed over time.

Government and Municipal Bonds. Bonds are instruments sold by the Federal, State, or Municipal organizations to raise funds for a particular project. These institutions give various Income Tax breaks as incentives for the public's participation. They carry some degree of safety while providing a decent rate of return. However, a penalty is assessed if they are redeemed prior to the date of maturity. This investment vehicle represents a viable way to save toward your offspring's education.

Corporate Stocks. Companies that are registered public entities offer shares of their stock for public investment. It would be wise to become familiar with the mission and vision (Prospectus) of a company, and with the quality of its leadership, before deciding to invest into its future. Here the risk factor increases – your profit or loss depends solely on the achievements of the company in the market place. The potential for a very high rate of return is possible. The reverse is also true – one can receive a low rate, and perhaps even lose your entire investment.

Real Estate Investments. In many circles it is believed that this can be the most lucrative venture. Perhaps because, unlike other investments, the potential for growth is almost certainly guaranteed. Even when there is a down turn in the economy, the patient real estate investor will eventually make a profit on the investment – patience is the key.

One can be an *active* or *passive* investor, or a combination of the two. In the former, it is necessary to obtain a license to buy and sell real estate property - selling at a price above the cost in order to make a profit. The rate of turn over (the time it took to sell the real estate after purchasing it) will impact how lucrative the venture turns out to be. In the latter, one simply purchases property, rents it out, and makes a profit from the monthly proceeds – all the while retaining ownership, and hence the value of the real estate.

Conclusion.

Investments represent a path toward financial freedom. Once it is done wisely, and is based on the investor's understanding of his or her own personality (Risk Tolerance Level), success is usually achieved. This should afford the freedom to turn to other areas of financial importance. The need to plan for Life Insurance is one such area.

Chapter 7

LIFE INSURANCE PLANNING

Much has been said of this vehicle toward financial emancipation. There are those who believe it is a waste of hard earned money, while others see its importance, and subscribe to one form or another. It will be necessary to examine the reason and purpose of Life Insurance in order to ascertain whether it's a viable enterprise.

What is Life Insurance? Many insurance companies have incorporated such a maze of explanations, that potential clients remain ignorant of the basic nature of insurance policies. ***Insurance is simply a financial instrument that is designed to provide financial relief after the experience of an injury, tragedy, or disaster. It should serve to restore the standard of living enjoyed prior to the incident.*** That's all it is, nothing more or less! This implies that one must be vigilant as a good steward, purchasing only what is really needed.

Insurance Policies – An Overview. It seems that there is an insurance policy to fit every need under the sun. There are those that are required by law, such as motor vehicle insurance, and others that are attached to various large loans, such as a mortgage. It follows therefore, that one needs to be careful when purchasing a policy – shopping around to ensure the best coverage for the cost.

There is no way to discuss all areas of insurance in this limited presentation. Consequently, I have chosen the basics of <u>Life</u> Insurance to establish a general guideline for the purchase of insurance policies. Many individuals shy away from this area of financial strategy – perhaps because it causes them to think of death. It would be a grave mistake to avoid planning for your financial future with the exclusion of a Life Insurance strategy. The need is greater during your youth, and declines as you grow older (providing you implemented sound financial planning in the early years).

Life Insurance. At this point there is a crucial observation based on the definition of insurance mentioned previously. Insurance becomes redundant and unnecessary when one acquires (inherits) or accumulates the equivalent funds necessary to maintain the current standard of living after an injury, tragedy, or disaster.

Many individuals procrastinate in the area of Life Insurance while they are young. Yet, this is the precise period in their lives when Life Insurance should be considered. Apart from being cheaper, it also provides a positive financial solution to the loss of income after the *premature* death of the main breadwinner. Much debt is usually incurred when one begins to raise a family – outstanding education costs, mortgage loans and such like, are at their highest. How will these be repaid in the absence of an alternate source of income after the 'passing' of the breadwinner? It is here that Life Insurance proves its worth, and demonstrates the wisdom of your early subscription.

Sound planning establishes a financial growth pattern based on a *goal* that enables the acquisition of adequate funds for your desired standard of living. These factors are at the helm of your choice of one of the two main types of insurance; *Term Life* or *Whole Life*.

Term Life Insurance.

Most Financial Planners agree that *Term Life* is the better instrument for life insurance – it affords greater flexibility and benefits for the cost of coverage. The theory of *Decreasing Responsibility* supports the choice of *Term* insurance – your financial obligations, and hence the need for insurance, should decline with age. It is no wonder that businesses and corporations that offer insurance coverage to their employees use Term Life Insurance as their preferred means of insurance coverage. One should purchase low cost *Term* insurance at a young age. This allows you to obtain more coverage than you will with other insurance vehicles. The additional benefit is that, because of the low cost, you may have funds remaining. This allows you to compliment your insurance by investing those funds in another area. Investing in Mutual Funds (mentioned previously) is a great compliment, and will help to maximize your financial potential.

The Four Types of Term Life Insurance. There are essentially four types of *Term Life Insurance,* each serving a particular need, based on your position in life's cycle:

1. **Annual Renewable Term**. The cost of this insurance rises yearly as the insured grows older. It is manageable in the early years, but becomes very expensive with the passage of time.
2. The **Level Term** *approach.* This policy is purchased for a specific period. The cost is averaged throughout the life of the policy – there is no rise or fluctuation in cost.
3. The **Modified Level Term** approach. Similar to Level Term. However, the first year premium is the highest for the duration of the policy - adjusted to include the usual expenses related to the policy. Thereafter, the cost is

lower and remains constant (Level) throughout the remaining years of the policy.
4. The **Decreasing Term** approach. Less protection is usually required as one grows older. This policy retains a Level cost (premium) throughout its duration, while decreasing the face value progressively over time.

Perhaps you may be wondering how to make the right choice for appropriate coverage at the least cost. The guideline is to assess the total cost of the policy over its life. That way you are able to choose the best value available for a good price.

Whole Life Insurance.

This type of policy suggests that one needs insurance protection for your entire life. It appears attractive because it combines a saving or investment aspect with the protection. Consequently, the cost is much more than that of *Term* because of these benefits.

Many individuals advocate *Term* as a better alternative. The consideration is this - if one takes the difference between the high premium of *Whole Life* and the low premium of *Term*, then purchase *Term* and invest the difference in separate and independent instruments apart from the policy, a greater rate of return is usually experienced on the investment. In other words you can save more by using this strategy.

Cash Value. Apart from the preceding observations, there are some other concerns about *Whole Life*. Some individuals use the savings portion of this policy for retirement purposes. Investing the funds independently affords a better accumulation for the later years.

Whole Life also allows loans from the Cash Value. But interest is charged on the repayment of the loan. In comparison, there is usually no charge of interest on withdrawals from independent investments. Additionally one needs to be aware that any outstanding balance on a loan usually decreases the amount available for death benefits.

Some Purchasing Considerations.

The wise steward considers the various benefits and costs before purchasing insurance. Some important guidelines are as follows:

1. Avoid purchasing *Mortgage Insurance* that is based solely on the outstanding mortgage – it's nothing more than Life Insurance.
2. Look out for unnecessary frills – they add to the cost. However an option to consider is one which retains your policy in good standing if you are disabled and unable to pay the premium.
3. Never buy more than one policy per family – there are additional fees and other expenses for each policy. If necessary, simply add 'Riders' to include family members such as children. Usually the coverage on the adults will provide such benefits.
4. Ensure that the value of the insurance is adequate enough to afford the desired protection. The need will vary from individual to individual. Nevertheless, a good guide would be **eight times your annual income**.

An Overview.

Life Insurance is only one aspect of your financial plan – albeit an important one. Your responsibility as a good steward is to ensure that you purchase the best vehicle for the lowest cost. This allows you to 'free' up funds for other forms of investment. Remember, the need for Life Insurance protection diminishes over time – providing you follow a sound financial plan to increase 'substance' over the years. Now that you have adequate insurance coverage, let's consider Estate Planning - the next phase in your financial plan.

Chapter 8

ESTATE PLANNING

Statistics have shown that two out of three Americans die *intestate* – they die without leaving a *will*. It is alarming that so many individuals downplay the importance of this crucial aspect of Estate Planning. It may be out of ignorance or from the false conviction that the value of your estate makes it unnecessary.

Death is inevitable. It would be wise to declare intentions for your estate prior to your passing. If not, someone else (the courts) will do it for you after your death. The absence of an estate plan leaves your survivors and your estate exposed to serious risks.

An *Estate Plan* provides the legal framework to protect your wishes as a legacy to your loved ones. It should therefore serve to ensure that the appropriate persons benefit from your estate, it should serve to minimize the cost of federal and state transfer taxes, and finally, it should include an asset ownership strategy that serves to reduce probate and administrative expenses as much as is legally possible. The instruments used for this purpose are **Wills** and **Trusts.**

<u>The Will.</u>

A will is an oral declaration or written instrument, to take effect upon death, whereby a person disposes of property or directs how it shall not be disposed of, disposes of his body or any part thereof, exercises a power, appoints a fiduciary or makes any other provision for the administration of his estate, and which is *revocable during his lifetime.* (Taken from New York's Estate, Powers, & Trusts Laws – E.P.T.L. 1-2.19 (a)).

The Trust.

This is the vehicle through which someone known as the *Grantor*, releases some or all of their assets to another person or institution known as the *Trustee*. The purpose is for the Trustee to hold and manage the property according to written instructions. The Trustee has the fiduciary responsibility to pay the income and principal at specified times to those indicated in the Trust as *Beneficiaries*.

Will or Trust?

The regulations governing wills and trusts are so complex that it may be difficult to prepare such documents personally – a competent attorney may be required. The decision is whether to use a will or a trust, or perhaps a combination of the two. Such a decision depends on the value of the estate and the desired goal. The influential factor that helps to determine your choice may revolve around a strategy to avoid as much taxes as legally possible. The following are some basic considerations:

1. A *Will* needs to be probated. It therefore incurs related filing fees. A separate fee is required for property held out of state. There is no such requirement for the *Living (Revocable) Trust*, hence no probate related fees.
2. Estate taxes for both the Will and the Trust are the same. However, with some types of Trusts, there are strategies to avoid the Gift Transfer Tax, and to maximize the Marital Exclusion deduction as well. This would indicate that the Trust may be a better instrument for tax purposes.

3. A Will requires periodic reviews and adjustments to ensure it reflects your current desires. You have complete management control of the assets in your Trust, and can effect changes as you deem fit.
4. It is relatively less costly to prepare a Will than to prepare a Living Trust.
5. After your passing, a Will becomes a public document. A Trust retains its privacy.
6. Whereas your assets are frozen by the courts during probate after your death, The Trust continues to function and releases income and principal according to the written instructions of the Trust.

Some Estate Planning Guidelines.

It is obvious at this point that Estate Planning involves many different choices, and therefore requires great depth of thought. It should also be obvious that because of this very complexity, this presentation can only serve as a basic guide. Below are six guidelines to aid in developing your Estate Plan:

1. The Net Worth Statement you prepared after reading chapter 2, serves as the starting point to plan your estate. Now you also need to consider your potential tax liability for your estate – depending on the instrument/s you chose (Will or Trust, or both).
2. Determine your objectives in order to devise an appropriate strategy. For example, do you wish the Church to be one of your beneficiaries? Then the best instrument to save taxes in many ways may be to create a *Charitable Remainder Trust*. There may be other objectives, such as enabling your survivors to retain their standard of living, to provide for your children's education, or to appoint your

approved guardian for your minor offspring. Whatever they are, you need to have them outlined. You can always make adjustments over time.

3. Next, you should determine whether you are competent to prepare your own Will, or should retain an attorney. If you do it yourself, it is advisable that you have an attorney review it. Once the probate court determines the validity of your Will, the Executor begins the task of carrying out your wishes. Note that the process can be time consuming, and fees can be substantial.

4. Consider a Living (Revocable) Trust – it can save much of the fees mentioned above, and either complement or replace a Will, depending on the complexity of your situation. If you create a Trust in lieu of a Will, then you should appoint a separate entity to be co-trustee – a bank, financial planner or trust company – you can retain management of the Trust.

5. Some individuals overlook the expenses that can affect their estate after death. Medical expenses incurred during the final moments, legal fees, accounting fees, funeral expenses, appraisal fees and executor's fees are a few. But provision can be made for these prior to death. This saves any financial hardship on survivors. For example one can pre-pay your burial expenses – open a Funeral Trust with an approved company. You save toward your final funeral expenses, while gaining interest from the Trust.

6. There is a proverbial statement indicating that death and taxes are sure things. But would you prefer the state and IRS to get your money in preference to your survivors? If not, then you must devise ways to minimize the tax burden on your estate. The Unified Estate and Gift Tax rule has an individual exclusion of $5,250,000 in 2013. There is

also an annual gift allowance of $14,000 per person or organization. This can be doubled if you and your spouse should make joint annual gifts. The result is that your estate would be reduced and hence your tax liability. Note that the new tax laws allow any unused portion of your individual exclusion to be transferred to your spouse on your passing.
7. Without doubt, your circumstances will change over time, and consequently the changes will affect your objectives. It would therefore be prudent to review your plan at least every three years. Any change that affects your Will or Trust would dictate a revision of these instruments. Developments such as the passing of a beneficiary, a lifestyle change, the birth of a child, or a positive or negative financial impact would require a careful review of your estate plan.

It is never too late to begin planning for the distribution of your estate. It certainly should bring you some peace to know that you have prepared for the future financial wellbeing of your loved ones. Now you can begin to plan for your *Retirement*.

Chapter 9

RETIREMENT PLANNING

The most opportune time to begin planning for your retirement is *now!* Why? Because the further you are away from retirement, the greater is your potential to attain financial security for yourself and family. The longer you wait to begin, the more funds you will need to invest in order to meet the same goal.

The laws governing money, such as *Inflation, The Time Value of Money*, and *Compounding,* all lend toward starting your Retirement Plan early. The first two dictate that the item you can purchase with a $1 today will require more than a $1 to purchase it in the future. However, the *Law of Compounding* provides a safeguard when you invest - income is generated over a specified period of time to offset those negative effects. Perhaps an example would help to illustrate this observation.

Dan and Gabe are both 22 years of age. They each determined that they will retire at age 62. Both recognize the importance of investing in order to amass the funds needed to retain their current standard of living after retirement. They also agree that an IRA is one of the better investment vehicles. Dan begins to make an annual contribution of $2,000 *immediately*, and does so for 7 years. Gabe, however, does not begin a similar contribution until he is 29 years of age, and continues until age 62. If they were each fortunate enough to obtain a 10% rate of return, it is amazing how Dan's earlier start turns out to be more lucrative:

    a. Dan contributes a total of $14,000. Gabe contributes a total of $68,000.

b. Compounding at 10% annually:
At age 62 Dan's account = $533,225 Gabe's account = $540,049.

Gabe contributed $54,000 more than Dan ($68,000 - $14,000), but only gained a difference of $6,824 at age 62. Clearly it would be wise to begin investing as early as possible.

Some Retirement Planning Guidelines.

Now that you are fully persuaded that an early plan for retirement is critical, you may ask, "What are some necessary features to consider?" Below are some guidelines:

1. Determine the actual value of your *current* estate. It's similar to your *Net Worth* as described in chapter 2.
2. Next, determine what your current estate should really be by multiplying the total household income by the age of the older spouse if married. The result is then divided by 10. For example, if the total household income is $60,000 and the age of the older person is 30, the current estate should value ($60,000 X 30)/10 = **$180,000**.
3. If the value of your actual estate is less than what it should be, you need a saving plan to eliminate the difference. Cut out the extra cup of coffee daily, prepare your own lunch rather than purchasing from the cafeteria, reduce expenditure on entertainment etc. In other words take control over those expenses that can be reduced, and use the savings toward closing the Net Worth deficit.
4. Determine the *approximate* value of your estate at retirement. Avoiding the complexity of Present and Future Value calculations, simply multiply the desired current

estate of $180,000 X 6. The result, $1,080,000. This takes into consideration the effects of inflation over time, as well as your need to fund various family projects such as education for the children. It also dictates a disciplined investment strategy.

5. Assess the various investment vehicles available:
   a. **_An IRA_** for one of the better tax shelters – preferably a ROTH IRA if your goal is to save on Estate Taxes. Otherwise, a Traditional IRA for greater flexibility to borrow during emergencies. Note, withdrawals must be made from the Traditional IRA by age 70 ½ to avoid a penalty. There is no such rule with the ROTH.
   b. **_Mutual Funds_**. A great avenue for investment without a requirement for personal management – invest and forget. **PAY YOURSELF FIRST** by authorizing a Mutual Fund Company to make automatic periodic withdrawals of a specific sum from your wages – **Time** and **Consistency** will reward you exceptionally. Note, your Mutual Funds portfolio is managed professionally by the Company you choose, and is Diversified according to your Risk Tolerance Level discussed previously.
   c. **_A Spiritual Living Trust_**. It is anticipated that this 'investment' of 10% of all new income will cause some great debate and discussion. I am simply referring to **Tithes and Offerings.** It is not to be confused with the traditional Living Trust mentioned earlier, a good worldly vehicle, but rather recognized as God's impeccable way of guaranteeing our financial and physical wellbeing continuously. This is the surest way of creating a continuous flow of pre and post retirement income. Its spiritual implications signify a

perpetual benefit similar to a *Remainder Trust Fund* – you enjoy benefits under the *Living Trust,* and after you pass on to be with the Lord, the Remainder flows to your beneficiaries just as you wished. A marvelous transaction that simply requires *faith and consistency.*

d. **Pre-need Funeral Trust.** It is a wonderful thing to know that at your passing, your beneficiaries will not have the added responsibility to fund, or be concerned about the cost of your interment. Although the proceeds from a Life Insurance policy may suffice to meet such expenses, it would be better if all of its proceeds could be left to beneficiaries for their discretionary use. Alternatively, if necessary, it can help to defray the cost of legal procedures to probate the Will, or to cover expenses related to the decedent's Estate, including Estate Taxes.

The *Pre-need Funeral Trust* is a marvelous instrument to cover funeral and interment expenses. Its beauty lies in the *Interest* it generates while you save toward your desired financial target. The strategy is to know the approximate cost of such expenses, add 10% to cover inflation and other contingencies, and begin saving as early as possible to attain your goal.

e. **The 401K or 403 Plans.** Many employers make these retirement saving plans available to their employees – some even match the contributions made by their staff. You should contribute the maximum amount allowed, and authorize pretax contributions to defer taxes.

f. **SEP and Keogh Plans.** These are retirement plans for the self-employed and their employees. They have similar advantages as the IRA. An added benefit is that contributions to these plans are viewed as an expense to the business, and consequently serve to reduce taxes. The only difference lies with the Keogh plan which has rigid administrative requirements. The SEP has no plan administration requirements.

6. Life changes affect the best of plans; a birth, untimely death, unexpected inheritance, will all have an impact on your economic situation. A periodic review of your goals and retirement plan is necessary. You should make pertinent adjustments with a minimum delay, thereby retaining your intent and schedule for a financially secure retirement.

Finally, the imperative need to adopt an early strategy for Personal Savings and Investments, becomes very clear when we consider that together they represent about 40% of retirement income. We cannot depend on the Government for Social Security benefits (about 20%) or our employer for a Pension (about 15%). The remaining 25% is unfortunately obtained through post retirement employment, and other miscellaneous ventures to generate income.

Our financial security depends on us, and our ability to make sensible decisions. We must maximize what we keep, and minimize what we expend. Toward that end we should engage every legitimate avenue to ensure that various related taxes are avoided, or at a minimum where possible. The next chapter will examine some relevant approaches to achieve this goal.

Chapter 10

TAXATION – GENERAL

Taxation is one of the most complex aspects of Financial Planning. It is impractical to attempt an inclusive discussion of all areas in this, or any other presentation. Consequently, the following guidelines represent a basic approach to minimize the tax liability. They focus on some legitimate strategies to reduce or totally eliminate the tax burden – specifically, when engaging the various savings and investment instruments mentioned earlier.

I cannot stress enough the need to consult a competent Financial Planner and, or, a Tax Attorney to ensure the intricacies of your financial plan are addressed efficiently. The following suggestions are pertinent, but not exhaustive.

Individual Income Taxes.

Savings and investments are generally made possible from income received as a result of individual employment. It would therefore be prudent to begin with the impact of taxes affecting such income before proceeding to other areas.

Dependent and Other Exclusions. Every year each individual is allowed personal exemptions and exclusions from taxes based on the level of income, marital status, number of dependents, age, and, or personal disabilities. These are known and anticipated annual benefits. This allows the completion of a W4 form authorizing the employer to withhold Federal and State taxes based on the *legitimate* exemptions claimed. If done properly, it should result in a balanced situation when Income Taxes are filed by April 15 of the following year. However, unexpected changes in tax laws during the year can affect the best of plans.

Income Tax preparation and filing can be as simple as the foregoing, or include additional considerations that raise the level of complexity. For example, **ownership of a home** opens the door for several other benefits through the opportunity to *Itemize* deductions. However, for this to be a viable approach, the total of all itemized deductions must be greater than the personal exemption *(Standard Deduction)* mentioned earlier – only one can be claimed, *Standard* or *Itemized*, not both.

The choice to Itemize deductions allows the introduction of Medical expenses, State Taxes paid, Interest, Real Estate Taxes, and inclusive Insurance paid on the home, Charitable Contributions, including Tithes and Offerings, and other miscellaneous items such as Union Dues, and the cost of Uniforms. It should be noted that some of these deductions depend on the excess over a percentage of the *Adjusted Gross Income*.

Some other deductions that should not be overlooked are, Tuition expenses or Credits, Energy Credits, First Time Home Buyer's Credit, Credit for Business Use of the home (be careful if the intention is to sell the home eventually), the cost of Property Damages or Casualties in excess of Insurance proceeds, and the Earned Income Credit when income falls below the minimum level allowed.

These are just some general areas to consider when planning to minimize the Income Tax burden. I have refrained from using figures for the various allowances because of the constant changes from year to year. Once more I encourage the reader to consult a Financial Planner or Tax Attorney for greater details, and a personal and customized plan tailored to meet your individual tax needs.

Deferred Taxes – IRA & 401K. The IRA and 401K plans are structured to provide sources of income at retirement. That is why there are stringent rules and penalties associated with early withdrawals. However, there are certain situations such as emergencies and hardships that meet the criteria for early withdrawals. Loans are also allowed for tuition purposes. The wonderful thing about this is that you are borrowing from, and repaying yourself.

The icing on the cake for these types of savings/investments is that you can *Deduct* each contribution from your gross wages, and pay the current taxes only on the remainder. Taxes on the amount deducted towards the **Traditional IRA** or 401K, are *Deferred* until retirement – at which time it is likely that you will be in a lower tax bracket, and hence pay less taxes than would have been due without *Deferability*. **Interest on the <u>Roth</u> IRA is not usually taxed.** Additionally, you can reduce your tax liability even further by *Rolling Over* the lump sum 401K proceeds at retirement to an *Annuity* – paying taxes only on your periodic withdrawals instead of on the lump sum.

Taxes – Savings & Money Market. It is regrettable that your attempt to save can result in taxes on the interest you receive. Note that the Money Market Accounts offered by banks are not the same as those offered by brokerage firms and other financial institutions – the former pays interest, while the latter (similar to Mutual Funds) pays dividends.

Each year the institutions you do business with are legally obligated to send you a 1099-INT form by January 31, indicating the interest you earned (in excess of $10) the previous year. The accumulated interest must be reported on your Income Tax return.

Taxes – Insurance Policies. The proceeds from Insurance Policies are not usually taxable. However, if you receive the distribution in installments, a portion of each distribution may be taxable. If the Insurance Policy pays dividends, they are usually taxable – unless they are used to pay your premium.

Mutual Funds & Money Market Taxes. Both investment instruments pay dividends. These proceeds are considered income, and therefore generally subject to Income Taxes. Reinvestment of the proceeds does not normally assist to reduce the tax liability, unless other intricate stipulations apply. The general guideline is that once the proceeds are actually or *constructively* made available for withdrawal, taxes are due – you have the right of withdrawal, and actually do so, or choose to reinvest rather than withdraw the funds. The strategies that can minimize taxes in these investments are beyond the scope of this book. Consulting a good Tax Accountant or Attorney familiar with the intricacies of these complex laws would in itself be a wise investment.

Wills, Trusts & Estate Taxes. One of the reasons many people opt to prepare Wills rather than Trusts may lie in the complexity and possibly expensive nature of the latter. However, as mentioned previously, Trusts have a greater potential to manoeuver funds, and hence to implement measures that minimize Income and Estate Taxes. To begin with, while Wills are subjected to Probate and other administrative fees, Trusts avoid such expenses.

The remainder of this section will therefore focus on *some* of the ways one can ease the tax burden on an Estate through Trusts that are properly prepared. The list below represents a few of the more common areas pertinent to the intent of this book – it is simply impossible to cover the vast arena of all tax saving Trusts and methods that are available:

1. **The Charitable Remainder Trust.** This Trust allows the owner (grantor) of property or money to make a donation to a recognized charitable institution. It is unique in that the owner is able to utilize the property and receive income from it while alive. Beneficiaries receive the income, and the charity receives the principal after a specific duration. The merit lies in a threefold tax benefit – the value of the property is removed from the estate, and consequently lessens estate taxes. Secondly, the grantor is able to claim a deduction on personal Income Tax Returns for the fair market value of interest earned. Finally, the grantor is able to avoid any capital gains tax that might accrue.
2. **The Marital Trust.** This trust seeks to ensure that provision is made for the economic wellbeing of the surviving spouse. The Federal Tax Laws allow an unlimited marital deduction from an estate to the surviving spouse. However, if one takes full advantage of the *total* deduction allowed, intending to avoid estate taxes, it should be known that such taxes are simply postponed until the death of the surviving spouse. That final estate would be

impacted by the full estate tax burden. A better strategy may be to arrange a Non-Marital Trust.

3. **The Non-Marital Trust.** This legal instrument seeks to provide an income stream for the surviving spouse as well as for beneficiaries such as offspring. For this reason it is known by different names such as *Credit Shelter Trust, Bypass Trust, and Family Trust.*

   One tax saving strategy is to place the <u>current</u> value of the *Unified Credit* allowed into the Trust, and utilize the remainder for the *Marital Deduction.* That way, both the Trust and the Marital Deduction avoid the estate tax. Additionally, and this is the benefit to the surviving spouse – the final estate also avoids estate taxes on the amount within the Trust. This benefit flows to the beneficiaries after the decease of the second spouse.

   Some tax advisors advocate a further consideration. They recognize the power of inflation, and the potential effect on taxes due from the estate of the surviving spouse (at least from the marital deduction amount). They therefore advise that the *grantor* arranges to have some taxes paid on the first estate, and so minimize the taxes that would be due from the second.

   Another consideration that can influence the formation of a Non-Marital Trust is the need to protect the interest of beneficiaries. For example, the surviving spouse may decide to remarry. This can present legal issues regarding the estate. However, if the original Non-Marital Trust is properly prepared, it can limit how much the surviving spouse can withdraw beyond the prescribed annual allowance. This safeguards the vested amount for the beneficiaries.

4. **The Living Trust (Inter Vivos).** This is one of the more popular trusts because it enables the grantor to play an active role during his or her life. The grantor, who can also be a co-trustee, has the ability to utilize the property and money as desired. This special position enables the grantor to distribute gifts annually, not to exceed the total amount allowed annually, or the total of the lifetime exclusion for the estate. Neither the grantor nor the beneficiaries of such gifts would be liable for Federal taxation on the amounts given.

   It can be said that this Trust has many of the attributes of a *Will*. However, as mentioned earlier, unlike the Will, it avoids probate and other administrative costs. Many of the other types of Trusts are bound by the stipulations in the *Living Trust*. Properly crafted to take advantage of the various exclusions, this Trust can greatly minimize, if not eliminate the need to pay estate taxes.

5. **The Unified Gift & Transfer Tax.** The IRS has instituted many new laws recently to increase the annual amount allowed for individual gifts. Currently (2013) a gift to any one person or entity should not exceed $14,000 per year. However, several gifts of $14,000, each to a different individual, can be made providing the total does not exceed the *Lifetime Unified Credit* of $5.25 million (2013). This latter figure affects the Unified Gift and Transfer amount that can be excluded from the estate of the decedent for estate tax purposes. Any gifts distributed will reduce the amount available for exclusion.

Money, Life, & You – Financial Planning, Pre & Post Marital.
(A Christian Overview)

With effect from 2011, the unused portion of the gift exclusion of an estate may be transferred and added to the exclusion amount of the surviving spouse.

The following deductions are excluded from your final estate:

a. The Marital Deduction.
b. The state death tax deduction.
c. Funeral expenses paid from your estate.
d. The charitable deduction.
e. Outstanding debts you owe at the time of death.

The following gifts are not taxable:

a. Gifts equal to or less than the annual exclusion amount ($14,000 for 2013).
b. Medical expenses or Tuition paid for another person directly to the medical institution or school.
c. Gifts to your spouse.
d. Gifts to political organizations for their use.
e. Gifts to charities.

Gift Splitting. Finally, this strategy allows a couple to make gifts that can exceed the annual amount allowed. For example, a married couple has a combined gift allowance of $28,000 annually. The husband gives $22,000 to his niece, and his wife gives $20,000 to her nephew. Once they _agree_ to split the gifts, the calculation for gift tax purpose would be viewed as $11,000 from the husband and $11,000 from the wife for the niece, and $10,000 from the wife and $10,000 from the husband toward the nephew. In no case did either exceed the individual gift allowance of $14,000 because they agreed to split the gifts. Each of them must file a gift tax return.

The Pre-paid Funeral Trust. This is a sound legal plan to provide for final expenses without utilizing the proceeds from insurance policies or other investments. The strategy lies in the fact that as a Trust it avoids probate, and the funds are therefore not frozen as they would be under a Will.

It has the flexibility that allows either a lump sum deposit, or installment contributions toward the total estimated cost of the entire funeral arrangement. The investment gains interest annually. Such income must be reported on your individual tax returns. After all funeral expenses are met, any residual amount in the Trust is credited to the decedent's estate. Note that your wishes for funeral arrangements can be documented in the Certificate issued by the Trust at the time it is initiated. Where possible it may be wise to indicate on the Certificate that the remainder should pass directly to a designated charity included in the estate. That helps to prevent the amount from inclusion as a taxable portion of the estate.

This Trust affords some amount of psychological tranquility to family members at the time of bereavement – they are spared the stress of being burdened with the related financial arrangements for the funeral.

IRS Publication 950 is a good source for further information. You can obtain other related forms such as Form 709 for gift taxes, Form 706, Publication 559 and Form 1041 for estate taxes. You may also need Form 1041QFT to report income from a

Qualified Funeral Trust. Generally, for a more detailed description and directions, visit the IRS website at www.irs.gov. There is always great merit in seeking the advice of a competent tax adviser or tax attorney.

EPILOGUE

Legend has it that just before he died, Alexander the Great called his generals and gave them his three final wishes. Whether or not this is true, the psychological content merits our reflection:

1. That his coffin should be borne by the best doctors.
2. That his wealth should be strewn along the funeral route – including gold, invaluable stones, and money.
3. Finally, that his hands should extend outside the coffin so that they could be seen clearly by everyone.

When asked to explain his strange request, it is reported that Alexander gave the following response:

1. The presence of the best doctors will serve to illustrate that even they do not possess the power to heal.

2. The presence of his physical wealth indicated that he no longer needed it – it was obtained on earth where it has value, but remains here since it has no value elsewhere.

3. The exposure of his empty hands served to demonstrate that he was leaving this world the same way he came into it – empty handed. He had come to the ultimate end, and therefore no longer had access to the most precious facet of life, Time – it is limited, we can create more wealth, but not more time.

4. When we dedicate our time to someone else, we are actually demonstrating love, because we can never regain that time. In essence we are actually giving that person a segment of our life!

5. Time represents the best gift you can share with anyone, especially family and friends.

It is doubtful that Alexander, a Greek, believed in one God. Nevertheless, since his tutor was Aristotle, it is reasonable to accept that he would have gained some impressions concerning the philosophy of God, Time, Love, and wealth. These reflections, legend or not, remain pertinent through the ages.

Eternity never ends. Time is just a fleeting moment used to chronicle natural events. Since our natural existence involves time, we should make every effort to utilize it according to godly principles. True wealth cannot be described in monetary terms since it hinges on our spiritual relationship with God. According to Jesus' directions, we should seek the Kingdom of God and His righteousness first, and all other things would be made available (Matt. 6:33). Nevertheless, we cannot ignore the role of money in our quest for economic stability while on this side of eternity. Jesus Himself also spoke about wise monetary stewardship and investments (Luke 19:12-26).

The man and woman seeking to engage a permanent union with each other must be cognizant of both the spiritual and natural requirements for a joyful marriage. Sound financial management is a key factor in preserving such an endeavor. Consequently, individuals must ensure that they are compatible partners for this short journey called life. The need to avoid being unequally yoked, dictates a sensible assessment of a potential partner. Putting emotions aside, the Pre-Marital questions listed in chapter 2 are structured to enable an honest look at each other. This can serve to identify serious conflicts of interest, and sound an alarm prior to entering a lifelong covenant of marriage.

Once a couple *enters* their marriage forearmed with the knowledge of their Net Worth, and a plan to enhance their financial position, the rest is a matter of resilience and patience. The guidelines in this book are structured toward the progressive implementation of financial strategies that result in a stable economic environment for the entire family throughout their natural lives. **May God Bless You Richly As You Embark On This Exciting And Rewarding Journey In Accordance With His Will And His Way.**

MARANATHA!

Bibliography

Christensen, Burke (April 1998). *Credit Shelter Trusts.* Bell, Boyd, & Lloyd. Chicago, IL.

Lochray, Paul, JD (October 1991). *The Financial Planner's Guide to Estate Planning.* Financial Times, Prentice Hall Books.

Nurse, Donald (September 2012). *Managing God's Finances.* Createspace.com/3991925.

Pape, Glenn. *Investment Basics: Who Needs Estate Planning? You Do.* Stages, Fall 1998.

Pennell, Jeffrey & Williamson, R. Mark (1997). *The Economics of Prepaying Wealth Transfer Tax.* Trusts and Estates.

Primerica Financial Services (1994). *The Solution: How You can Take Control of Your Financial Life.* Primerica, Inc., Duluth, GA.

The Internal Revenue Service (2013). *Publication 950.* Retrieved from www.irs.gov on 10/30/2013.

Treasured Words – Alexander the Great. Extracted from; Guyaneseonline.wordpress.com on 11/19/2013.

www.ingramcontent.com/pod-product-compliance
Lightning Source LLC
Chambersburg PA
CBHW071806170526
45167CB00003B/1189